D0534837

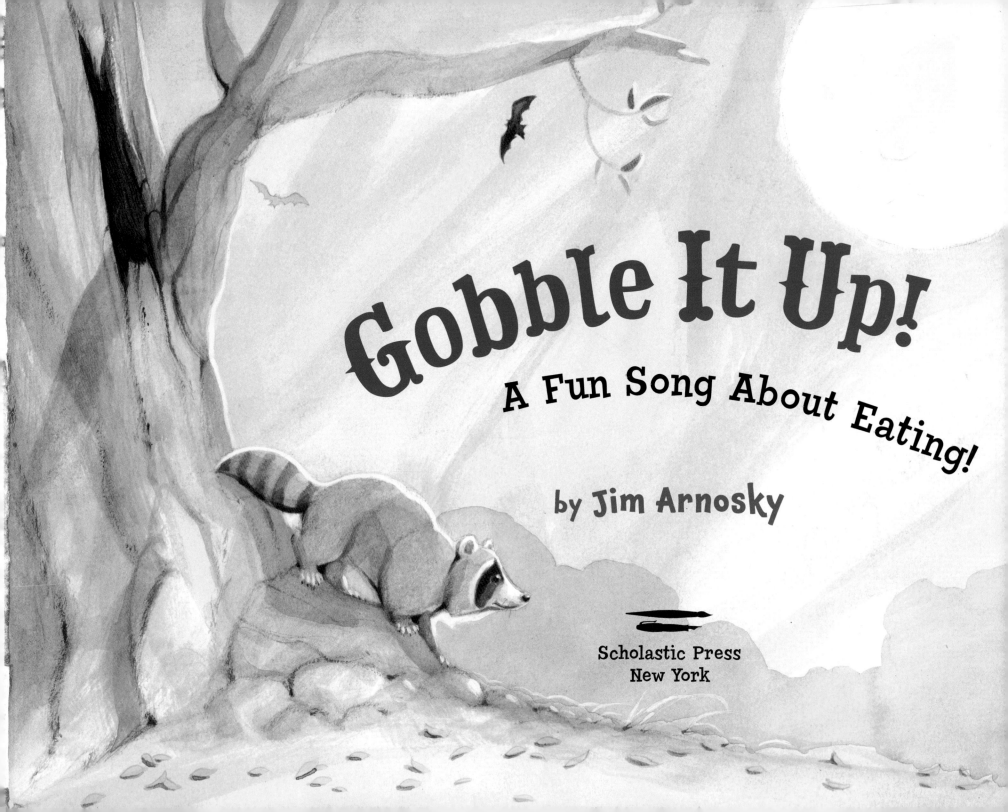

Gobble It Up!

A Fun Song About Eating!

by Jim Arnosky

Scholastic Press
New York

10 9 8 7 6 5 4 3 2 1   08 09 10 11 12

Printed in Singapore   46
First edition, September 2008

The text was set in Chowderhead.
The art was created using acrylic paint in a semi-opaque style on
acid-free watercolor paper.
Book design by Becky Terhune, Kay Petronio and Susan Schultz

Library of Congress Cataloging-in-Publication Data

Arnosky, Jim.
Gobble it up!: a fun song about eating! / by Jim Arnosky. – 1st ed.
    p. cm.
Summary: Rhyming text invites the reader to imagine being a hungry
raccoon, crocodile, shark, whale, or panda bear while learning what
each creature enjoys eating.
ISBN-13: 978-0-439-90362-2
ISBN-10: 0-439-90362-9
[1. Animals—Food—Fiction. 2. Food habits—Fiction. 3. Food chains
(Ecology)—Fiction. 4. Stories in rhyme.] I. Title.

PZ8.3.A648Gob 2008
[E]—dc22
2007029510

For Jacquelyn,
Gabriella,
and Delaney

If you were a wild raccoon,

you'd hunt at night by the light of the moon.

You'd catch some crawdads where they crawl . . .

Yes, you would. Yes, you would.
You'd crunch up crawdads all you could.
Yes, you would. Yes, you would.
You'd gobble them up and they'd taste good!

If you were a crocodile, you'd fool those ducklings with your smile.

When they'd swim by for a closer look . . .

Yes, you would. Yes, you would.
You'd eat those ducklings if you could!

Yes, you would. Yes, you would. You'd gobble them up and they'd taste good!

That's the way we all survive.
We gobble food to stay alive.
We eat the food we have, and then—

we have to hunt for food again!

If you were a **great white shark,**
you'd cruise the shallows after dark.

You'd circle fishes in their schools . . .
. . . and gobble them up, two by two!

Yes, you would. Yes, you would. You'd chomp up fishes all you could.

Yes, you would. Yes, you would. You'd **gobble them up** and they'd taste **good!**

If a great whale you could be,

you'd dive to the bottom

You'd pick a fight with the biggest kid . . .

of the deep blue sea.

. . . and gobble you up **a giant squid!**

Yes, you would. Yes, you would.
You'd eat that squid up if you could.

Yes, you would. Yes, you would.
You'd gobble it up and it'd taste good!

If you were a panda bear, you couldn't live just anywhere.

You'd have to find a place where you could feed all day on rare bamboo!

Yes, you would. Yes, you would.
You'd eat the last shoot if you could.

Yes, you would. Yes, you would.

You'd gobble it up and it'd taste good!

That's the way we all survive.
We gobble food to stay alive.
We eat the food we have, and then—

We have to hunt for food again!